POWER BI, DATA VISUALIS

INTERVIEW QUESTIONS FOR PLAC...

PROGRESSION

1. What is a slicer in Power BI?
    a) A visual element used to filter data in a report.
    b) A type of chart used to display trends in data over time.
    c) A function used to calculate the average of a set of values
Answer: a

2. Which language is used to write custom calculations in Power BI?
    a) C++
    b) Python
    c) DAX

Answer: c

3. What is a measure in Power BI?
    a) A calculation used to aggregate data in a report.
    b) A visual element used to filter data in a report.
    c) A type of chart used to display trends in data over time.
Answer: a

4. What is the purpose of Power Query in Power BI?
    a) To transform and clean data before it is loaded into a report.
    b) To create custom visuals for a report.
    c) To create interactive dashboards for end-users

    Answer: a

5. Which type of chart is used to compare values across categories in
    Power BI?
    a) Pie chart.
    b) Line chart.
    c) Bar chart
    Answer: c.

6. What is the purpose of Power Query in Power BI?
    a) To transform and clean data before it is loaded into a report.
    b) To create custom visuals for a report.
    c) To create interactive dashboards for end-users
Answer: a

7. Which type of chart is used to compare values across categories in Power BI?
   a) Pie chart.
   b) Line chart
   c) Bar chart
Answer: c

8. What is a hierarchy in Power BI?
   a) A way of organizing data by levels of granularity.
   b) A visual element used to filter data in a report.
   c) A type of chart used to display trends in data over time
Answer: a

9. What is a drill-through in Power BI?
   a) The ability to navigate from one report to another based on a selected data point.
   b) The ability to filter data in a report based on a selected data point.
   c) The ability to export data from a report to another application
Answer: a

10. What is the purpose of the Power BI service?
    a) To publish and share reports with other users.
    b) To create custom visuals for a report.
    c) To transform and clean data before it is loaded into a report
Answer: a

11. What is a calculated column in Power BI?
    a) A column in a table created by a formula.
    b) A visual element used to filter data in a report.
    c) A type of chart used to display trends in data over time
Answer: a

12. What is a matrix visual in Power BI?
    a) A visual element used to display data in rows and columns, with aggregate values in the intersections.
    b) A type of chart used to display trends in data over time.
    c) A visual element used to filter data in a report
Answer: a

3. What is Power BI?
   a) A suite of business analytics tools from Microsoft to analyze data and share insights
   b) A programming language for statistical analysis.
   c) A database management system for storing and retrieving data.
   d) A type of cloud computing service

Answer: a

4. What are the main components of Power BI?
   a) Power BI Desktop, Power BI Service, and Power BI Mobile.
   b) Power Query, Power Pivot, and Power View.
   c) Excel, SharePoint, and SQL Server.
   d) Windows, iOS, and Android

Answer: a

5. What is Power Query in Power BI?
   a) A data transformation and cleansing tool.
   b) A data visualization tool.
   c) A data modeling tool.
   d) A data analysis tool

Answer: a

6. What is Power Pivot in Power BI?
   a) A data modeling and analysis tool.
   b) A data visualization tool.
   c) A data transformation tool.
   d) A data integration tool

Answer: a

7. What is Power View in Power BI?
   a) A data visualization tool for creating interactive reports and dashboards.
   b) A data transformation tool.
   c) A data modeling tool.
   d) A data analysis tool

Answer: a

18. What is DAX in Power BI?
    a) A formula language for creating custom calculations in Power Pivot
    b) A data transformation tool.
    c) A data modeling tool.
    d) A data visualization tool

Answer: a

19. What is a visual in Power BI?
    a) A chart, table, or other graphical representation of data.
    b) A programming language for statistical analysis.
    c) A database management system for storing and retrieving data.
    d) A type of cloud computing service

Answer: a

20. What is a dashboard in Power BI?
    a) A single-page view of important metrics and data visualizations.
    b) A database management system for storing and retrieving data.
    c) A data modeling tool.
    d) A type of cloud computing service

Answer: a

21. What is a report in Power BI?
    a) A collection of visuals and data visualizations.
    b) A data modeling tool.
    c) A data transformation tool.
    d) A database management system for storing and retrieving data

Answer: a

22. What is the Power BI service?
    a) A cloud-based service for publishing, sharing, and collaborating on Power BI content.
    b) A data transformation tool.
    c) A data modeling tool.
    d) A data visualization tool

Answer: a

3. What is the Power BI mobile app?
   a) A mobile app for accessing and interacting with Power BI content on the go.
   b) A data modeling tool.
   c) A data transformation tool.
   d) A data visualization tool

nswer: a

4. What is the Power BI gateway?
   a) A tool for connecting on-premises data sources to Power BI in the cloud.
   b) A data transformation tool.
   c) A data modeling tool.
   d) A data visualization tool

nswer: a

5. What types of data sources can be used with Power BI?
   a) Excel, SQL Server, SharePoint, and many others.
   b) Power Query, Power Pivot, and Power View.
   c) Python, R, and MATLAB.
   d) Windows, iOS, and Android

answer: a

6. What is a slicer in Power BI?
   a) A visual control that filters data based on user selection.
   b) A type of chart that displays data as a series of bars.
   c) A method for joining tables in Power BI.
   d) None of the above

Answer: a) A visual control that filters data based on user selection

27. Which language is used to write custom calculations and queries in Power BI?
   a) R   b) Python   c) SQL   d) DAX

Answer: d) DAX

28. What is a dashboard in Power BI?
    a) A single page that displays visualizations and insights based on dat
    from multiple sources.
    b) A data storage component in Power BI
    c) A type of chart that displays data as a series of bars.
    d) None of the above

Answer: a) A single page that displays visualizations and insights based c
data from multiple sources

29. Which of the following is a Power BI desktop component?
    a) Power BI Report Server
    b) Power BI Service.
    c) Power BI Mobile App.
    d) Power Query Editor

Answer: d) Power Query Editor

30. What is a measure in Power BI?
    a) A calculation used to aggregate and analyze data
    b) A type of visual used to display data
    c) A method for joining tables in Power BI.
    d) None of the above

Answer: a) A calculation used to aggregate and analyze data

31. Which of the following is a method for sharing Power BI content with
    others?
    a) Embedding a report or dashboard in a website or application
    b) Creating a copy of the report or dashboard and emailing it to others
    c) Saving the report or dashboard as a PDF and sharing it through a fi
    sharing service
    d) None of the above

Answer: a) Embedding a report or dashboard in a website or application

32. Which of the following is a Power BI service component?
    a) Power BI Desktop.
    b) Power BI Report Server.
    c) Power BI Mobile App.
    d) Power Query Editor

Answer: c) Power BI Mobile App

33. What is the purpose of the Power Query Editor in Power BI?
   a) To transform and clean data before it is loaded into a data model
   b) To create visualizations and reports based on data in a data model
   c) To create custom calculations using DAX.
   d) None of the above

Answer: a) To transform and clean data before it is loaded into a data model

34. What is the purpose of the Power BI service?
   a) To publish, share, and collaborate on Power BI content in the cloud
   b) To create and design visualizations and reports in Power BI
   c) To manage data sources used in Power BI
   d) None of the above

Answer: a) To publish, share, and collaborate on Power BI content in the cloud

35. Which of the following is a type of visual that can be created in Power BI?
   a) Line chart   b) Scatter chart
   c) Treemap   d) All of the above

Answer: d) All of the above

36. What is a drill-through in Power BI?
a) A method for navigating to more detailed information within a report
b) A type of visual that displays data as a series of bars
c) A method for joining tables in Power BI
d) None of the above

Answer: a) A method for navigating to more detailed information within a report

37. What is a slicer in Power BI?
 a) A visual element used to filter data based on selected criteria
 b) A type of chart used to display trends over time
 c) A feature used to highlight data points in a chart
 d) A tool used to create and manage relationships between tables

Answer- a) A visual element used to filter data based on selected criteria

38. What is the purpose of a measure in Power BI?
    a) To perform calculations based on data in a table or column.
    b) To group data based on selected criteria
    c) To filter data based on a user's selection
    d) To create a new table from existing data in multiple tables

Answer- a) To perform calculations based on data in a table or column

39. How does Power BI integrate with Excel?
    a) By allowing users to import data from Excel into Power BI.
    b) By allowing users to export reports and visuals from Power BI to Excel
    c) By allowing users to edit Power BI visuals in Excel.
    d) All of the above.

Answer- d) All of the above

40. What is a visual-level filter in Power BI?
    a) A filter that applies to an individual visual or chart.
    b) A filter that applies to an entire page or report.
    c) A filter that applies to all visuals in a report.
    d) A filter that applies to data at the table or column level

Answer- a) A filter that applies to an individual visual or chart

41. How can you create a custom visual in Power BI?
    a) By importing a visual created by another user or organization.
    b) By using the developer tools in Power BI to create a new visual.
    c) By modifying an existing visual in Power BI.
    d) Custom visuals cannot be created in Power BI

Answer- b) By using the developer tools in Power BI to create a new visual

42. What is the Power BI Report Server?
    a) An on-premises solution for publishing, managing, and delivering Power BI reports.
    b) A cloud-based solution for data visualization and analysis.
    c) A data storage solution for Power BI datasets.
    d) None of the above

Answer- a) An on-premises solution for publishing, managing, and delivering Power BI reports

43. What is a slicer in Power BI? a) A visual element that allows users to filter data in a report.
    b) A function that creates a calculated column in a dataset.
    c) A measure that calculates the difference between two values in a dataset.
    d) None of the above

Answer- a) A visual element that allows users to filter data in a report

44. What is the Power BI mobile app?
    a) A mobile application for accessing and interacting with Power BI reports on-the-go.
    b) A desktop application for creating and editing Power BI reports.
    c) A web-based interface for sharing and collaborating on Power BI reports.
    d) None of the above.

Answer- a) A mobile application for accessing and interacting with Power BI reports on-the-go

45. What is the difference between a measure and a calculated column in Power BI?
   a) A measure is a calculation based on a single column, while a calculated column is based on multiple columns.
   b) A measure is an aggregated value, while a calculated column is a new column added to a table.
   c) A measure is used for filtering data, while a calculated column is used for sorting data.
   d) None of the above

Answer- b) A measure is an aggregated value, while a calculated column is a new column added to a table

46. What is the Power BI service?
   a) A cloud-based solution for publishing, sharing, and collaborating on Power BI reports.
   b) A desktop application for creating and editing Power BI reports.
   c) An on-premises solution for managing and delivering Power BI reports.
   d) None of the above

Answer- a) A cloud-based solution for publishing, sharing, and collaborating on Power BI reports

47. What is the Power Query Editor in Power BI?
   a) A tool for transforming and cleaning data before importing it into Power BI.
   b) A tool for creating and managing dashboards in Power BI.
   c) A tool for creating calculated columns and measures in Power BI.
   d) None of the above

Answer- a) A tool for transforming and cleaning data before importing it into Power BI

8. What is a hierarchy in Power BI?
   a) A way of organizing data into levels of detail and summarization b) A way of visualizing data using a tree structure c) A way of filtering data using multiple criteria d) None of the above

nswer- a) A way of organizing data into levels of detail and ummarization

9. What is a Quick Measure in Power BI?
   a) A pre-built calculation that can be added to a report b) A way of creating a custom visual in Power BI c) A way of importing data from an external source into Power BI d) None of the above

nswer- a) A pre-built calculation that can be added to a report

0. What is the DAX language in Power BI?
   a) A formula language used to create custom calculations and measures
   b) A scripting language used to automate tasks in Power BI
   c) A programming language used to create custom visuals in Power BI
   d) None of the above

Answer- a) A formula language used to create custom calculations and measures

51. What is a drill-through in Power BI?
a) A way of navigating from a summary report to a detailed report.
b) A way of filtering data using a slider or range control.
c) A way of visualizing data using a heatmap or tree map.
d) None of the above
Answer- a) A way of navigating from a summary report to a detailed report

1) What is data visualization?

a) The graphical representation of data to help users better understand and analyze information.

b) The process of analyzing data.

c) The process of collecting data.

d) The process of transforming data into information

Answer: a) The graphical representation of data to help users better understand and analyze information

2) What is the primary goal of data visualization?

a) To communicate complex data in a clear and effective manner.

b) To collect and organize data.

c) To analyze data

d) To store data in a database

Answer: a) To communicate complex data in a clear and effective manner

3) What are some common types of data visualizations?

a) Bar charts, line charts, scatter plots, and heat maps.

b) SQL, Python, Java, and C++

c) Pie charts, histograms, and box plots.

d) Machine learning, natural language processing, and neural networks

Answer: a) Bar charts, line charts, scatter plots, and heat maps

4) What is the purpose of adding analytics to data visualization?

a) To provide deeper insights and understanding of the data being visualized.

b) To make the data more aesthetically pleasing.

c) To help store and manage the data more effectively.

d) To speed up the data visualization process

Answer: a) To provide deeper insights and understanding of the data being visualized

5) What is the difference between descriptive and predictive analytics?
a) Descriptive analytics provides insights into what happened in the past, while predictive analytics uses historical data to make future predictions.

b) Descriptive analytics is used for machine learning, while predictive analytics is used for natural language processing.

c) Descriptive analytics is used for sentiment analysis, while predictive analytics is used for image recognition

d) Descriptive analytics is used for data visualization, while predictive

analytics is used for data collection

Answer: a) Descriptive analytics provides insights into what happened in the past, while predictive analytics uses historical data to make future predictions

6) What is a dashboard?

a) A visual display of key performance indicators and other important data.

b) A data visualization technique used for sentiment analysis.

c) A type of neural network used for image recognition

d) A machine Learning algorithm used for data classification

Answer: a) A visual display of key performance indicators and other important data

7) What is the purpose of data storytelling in data visualization?

a) To help users understand the context and meaning behind the data being visualized.

b) To add more complex visualizations to the data.

c) To make the data more aesthetically pleasing.

d) To help store and manage the data more effectively

Answer: a) To help users understand the context and meaning behind the data being visualized

8) What is the importance of color in data visualization?

a) Color can be used to highlight important information and make data more visually appealing.

b) Color has no impact on the effectiveness of data visualization.

c) Color can be used to store and manage data more effectively.

d) Color can speed up the data visualization process

Answer: a) Color can be used to highlight important information and make data more visually appealing

9) What is a data visualization tool?

a) A software application used for creating visual representations of data.

b) A database management system.

c) A programming language

d) A machine learning algorithm

Answer: a) A software application used for creating visual representations of data

10)   What is a heat map in data visualization?

a) A graphical representation of data using colors to represent values.

b) A diagram that shows the relationships between different variables.

c) A scatter plot with a line of best fit.

d) A visual representation of hierarchies or relationships between elements

Answer: a) A graphical representation of data using colors to represent values

11)   What is a box plot in data visualization?

a) A graphical representation of data using colors to represent values

b) A diagram that shows the relationships between different variables
c) A scatter plot with a line of best fit.

d) A visual representation of statistical data that shows the distribution of a dataset.

Answer: d) A visual representation of statistical data that shows the distribution of a dataset.

12)	What is a scatter plot in data visualization?
13)	a) A diagram that shows the relationships between different variables.

b) A visual representation of hierarchies or relationships between elements.

c) A graphical representation of data using colors to represent values.

d) A visual representation of statistical data that shows the distribution of a dataset.

Answer: a) A diagram that shows the relationships between different variables

14)	What is a tree map in data visualization?

a) A visual representation of hierarchies or relationships between elements.

b) A graphical representation of data using colors to represent values

c) A scatter plot with a line of best fit.

d) A visual representation of statistical data that shows the distribution of a dataset.

Answer: a) A visual representation of hierarchies or relationships between elements.

15)	What is a funnel chart in data visualization?

a) A visual representation of a process that narrows down a large number of options to a smaller number.

b) A diagram that shows the relationships between different variables

c) A graphical representation of data using colors to represent values.

d) A visual representation of statistical data that shows the distribution of a dataset.

Answer: a) A visual representation of a process that narrows down a large number of options to a smaller number

16)   What is a stacked bar chart in data visualization?.

a) A graphical representation of data that shows the comparison of different variables using horizontal or vertical bars.

b) A visual representation of hierarchies or relationships between elements

c) A scatter plot with a line of best fit.

d) A visual representation of statistical data that shows the distribution of a dataset.

Answer: a) A graphical representation of data that shows the comparison of different variables using horizontal or vertical bars

17)   What is a line chart in data visualization?

a) A graphical representation of data that shows the trend of a variable over time

b) A diagram that shows the relationships between different variables

c) A scatter plot with a line of best fit.

d) A visual representation of statistical data that shows the distribution of a dataset.

Answer: a) A graphical representation of data that shows the trend of a variable over time

18)   What is a spider chart in data visualization?

a) A visual representation of data that compares multiple variables using a radial axis

b) A diagram that shows the relationships between different variables

c) A graphical representation of data using colors to represent values.

d) A visual representation of statistical data that shows the distribution of a dataset.

Answer: a) A visual representation of data that compares multiple variables using a radial axis

19)   What is a word cloud in data visualization?

a) A visual representation of text data that displays words in different sizes based on their frequency

b) A visual representation of hierarchies or relationships between elements

c) A graphical representation of data using colors to represent values.

d) A visual representation of statistical data that shows the distribution of a dataset.

Answer: a) A visual representation of text data that displays words in different sizes based on their frequency.

20)   What is a histogram in data visualization?

a) A visual representation of statistical data that shows the distribution of a dataset

b) A diagram that shows the relationships between different variables

c) A graphical representation of data using colors to represent values

d) A visual representation of hierarchies or relationships between elements.

Answer: a) A visual representation of statistical data that shows the distribution of a dataset

21)   What is a pie chart in data visualization?

a) A graphical representation of data that shows the proportion of different categories in a dataset.

b) A visual representation of hierarchies or relationships between elements

c) A scatter plot with a line of best fit

d) A visual representation of statistical data that shows the distribution of a dataset.

Answer: a) A graphical representation of data that shows the proportion of different categories in a dataset

22)   What is the purpose of data visualization?

a) To help users better understand and interpret complex data.

b) To collect data from various sources.

c) To store and manage data in a database.

d) None of the above

Answer: a) To help users better understand and interpret complex data

23)   What is a heat map in data visualization?

a) A type of chart that uses color to represent values.

b) A tool used to measure the temperature of data

c) A type of algorithm used in machine learning

d) None of the above

Answer: a) A type of chart that uses color to represent values

24)   What is a scatter plot in data visualization?

a) A type of chart that uses dots to represent values.

b) A tool used to measure air pollution

c) A type of machine learning model

d) None of the above

Answer: a) A type of chart that uses dots to represent values

25)   What is a tree map in data visualization?

a) A type of chart that uses rectangles to represent values.

b) A tool used to measure the growth of trees.

c) A type of statistical analysis.

d) None of the above

Answer: a) A type of chart that uses rectangles to represent values

26)   What is a histogram in data visualization?

a) A type of chart that displays the frequency of values in a data set

b) A tool used to measure distance

c) A type of machine learning algorithm.

d) None of the above

Answer: a) A type of chart that displays the frequency of values in a data set

27)   What is a line chart in data visualization?

a) A type of chart that displays data points connected by a line

b) A tool used to measure angles

c) A type of database management system

d) None of the above

Answer: a) A type of chart that displays data points connected by a line

28)   What is a pie chart in data visualization?

a) A type of chart that displays data as slices of a pie.

b) A tool used to measure volume.

c) A type of machine learning model

d) None of the above

Answer: a) A type of chart that displays data as slices of a pie

29)   What is a bar chart in data visualization?

a) A type of chart that displays data as bars.

b) A tool used to measure weight.

c) A type of algorithm used in natural language processing

d) None of the above

30) What is a box plot in data visualization?

a) A type of chart that displays the distribution of values in a data set

b) A tool used to measure temperature

c) A type of machine learning model

d) None of the above

Answer: a) A type of chart that displays the distribution of values in a data set

31) What is a violin plot in data visualization?

a) A type of chart that combines a box plot and a density plot.

b) A tool used to measure sound intensity.

c) A type of algorithm used in image recognition.

d) None of the above

Answer: a) A type of chart that combines a box plot and a density plot

32) What is a word cloud in data visualization?

a) A type of chart that displays words in different sizes based on their frequency in a data set.

b) A tool used to measure the speed of a computer

c) A type of statistical analysis.

d) None of the above

Answer: a) A type of chart that displays words in different sizes based on their frequency in a data set

33)   What is a dashboard in data visualization?

a) A collection of visualizations and metrics used to monitor and analyze data

b) A tool used to measure the brightness of a screen.

c) A type of database management system d) None of the above

Answer: a) A collection of visualizations and metrics used to monitor d analyze data.

34)   What is data exploration in data visualization?

a) The process of using visualizations to identify patterns and insights in data.

b) The process of collecting data from various sources

c) The process of storing and managing data in a database.

d) None of the above

Answer: a) The process of using visualizations to identify patterns and insights in data.

35)   What is data storytelling in data visualization?

a) The process of using visualizations to tell a story with data.

b) The process of creating visualizations without context or narrative.

c) The process of collecting and storing data in a database.

d) None of above.

Answer: a) The process of using visualizations to tell a story with data

36) What is a heatmap in data visualization?

a) A graphical representation of data using colors to represent values

b) A chart that displays data in a hierarchical structure.

c) A type of scatter plot that shows the relationship between two variables.

d) None of the above

Answer: a) A graphical representation of data using colors to represent values

37) What is a tree map in data visualization?

a) A type of chart that displays data in a hierarchical structure using rectangles

b) A type of chart that displays data over time

c) A type of chart that displays data using different shapes.

d) None of the above

Answer: a) A type of chart that displays data in a hierarchical structure using rectangles.

38) What is a Sankey diagram in data visualization?

a) A type of chart that shows the flow of data or information between different entities.

b) A type of chart that displays data over time.

c) A type of chart that displays data using different shapes.

d) None of the above

Answer: a) A type of chart that shows the flow of data or information between different entities.

39)   What is a parallel coordinates plot in data visualization?

a) A type of chart that displays multivariate data by plotting each variable on a separate axis.

b) A type of chart that displays data over time.

c) A type of chart that displays data using different shapes.

d) None of the above

Answer: a) A type of chart that displays multivariate data by plotting each variable on a separate axis

40)   What is a word cloud in data visualization?

a) A graphical representation of text data in which the size of each word indicates its frequency or importance.

b) A chart that displays data in a hierarchical structure.

c) A type of chart that displays data using different shapes.

d) None of the above

Answer: a) A graphical representation of text data in which the size of each word indicates its frequency or importance

41)   What is the purpose of data visualization in analytics?

a) To present data in a way that is easy to understand and interpret.

b) To create visual interest in reports and presentations.

c) To make data look more attractive.

d) None of the above

Answer: a) To present data in a way that is easy to understand and interpret

42)   What is the benefit of using data visualization in analytics?

a) It allows for better decision making by enabling users to identify patterns and trends in data

b) It can help to reduce errors in data analysis

c) It can save time by making it easier to explore and understand large datasets

d) All of the above

Answer: d) All of the above

43)   What are some common tools used for data visualization in analytics?

a) Tableau, Power BI, and Excel.

b) SQL, Python, and R.

c) Java, C++, and Ruby

d) None of the above

Answer: a) Tableau, Power BI, and Excel

44)   What is the importance of color in data visualization?

a) It can be used to highlight important information and make data easier to understand

b) It has no impact on the effectiveness of data visualization

c) It can be distracting and should be avoided.

d) None of the above

Answer: a) It can be used to highlight important information and make data easier to understand

45)   What is the difference between a bar chart and a histogram?

a) A bar chart displays categorical data, while a histogram displays continuous data.

b) A bar chart displays continuous data, while a histogram displays categorical data.

c) There is no difference between a bar chart and a histogram.

d) A bar chart displays data in a 3D format, while a histogram displays data in 2D format.

Answer: a) A bar chart displays categorical data, while a histogram displays continuous data.

46)   What is a box plot in data visualization?

a) A graphical representation of data using quartiles to show the spread and skewness of the data.

b) A chart that displays data in a hierarchical structure.

c) A type of scatter plot that shows the relationship between two variables.

d) None of the above

Answer: d) A visual representation of statistical data that shows the spread and skewness of the data

47)   What is the purpose of labeling in data visualization?

a) To provide context and explanation for the data being presented.

b) To make the visualization look more attractive.

c) To provide a legend for the chart.

d) None of the above

Answer: a) To provide context and explanation for the data being presented

48)   What is the purpose of data visualization?

a) To present data in a visual and understandable way.

b) To collect data from various sources.

c) To store data for future analysis.

d) To transform data into different formats.

Answer: (a) To present data in a visual and understandable way.

1. What does SaaS stand for?

Answer: Software as a Service.

2. Which of the following is not a benefit of SaaS?

   a. Cost-effectiveness.

   b. Scalability.

   c. Flexibility.

   d. Local installation

Answer: d. Local installation.

3. Which of the following is a popular SaaS application used for project management?

   a. Slack.

   b. Asana.

   c. Trello

   d. Zoom

Answer: b. Asana.

4. Which of the following is an example of a SaaS platform for customer relationship management?

   a. Salesforce

   b. Oracle.

c. Microsoft Dynamics.

d. SAP

Answer: a. Salesforce.

5. Which of the following is a common concern when it comes to SaaS?

   a. Security

   b. Cost

   c. Scalability

   d. Compatibility

Answer: a. Security.

6. What is the main advantage of SaaS over traditional software installations?

   a. Scalability.

   b. Cost-effectiveness

   c. Flexibility

   d. All of the above

Answer: d. All of the above.

7. Which of the following is a characteristic of SaaS?

   a. Local installation

   b. On-premise hosting

c. Subscription-based pricing

d. Perpetual licensing

Answer: c. Subscription-based pricing.

8. Which of the following is a potential disadvantage of SaaS?

a. Limited customization

b. Higher upfront costs

c. Longer implementation time

d. Higher maintenance costs

Answer: a. Limited customization.

9. Which of the following is a popular SaaS application used for online document collaboration?

a. Dropbox

b. OneDrive

c. Google Docs

d. Box

Answer: c. Google Docs.

10.   What is the main advantage of SaaS for small businesses?

a. Scalability

b. Cost-effectiveness

c. Flexibility

d. All of the above

Answer: d. All of the above.

11.   Which of the following is a potential disadvantage of SaaS for large businesses?

a. Limited customization

b. Higher upfront costs

c. Longer implementation time

d. Limited scalability

Answer: d. Limited scalability.

12.   Which of the following is an example of a SaaS platform for human resources management?

a. Workday

b. Oracle

c. SAP SuccessFactors

d. ADP

Answer: a. Workday.

13.   Which of the following is a potential advantage of SaaS over traditional software installations?

a. Lower upfront costs

b. More customization options

c. Faster implementation time

d. Local installation

4. Which of the following is a characteristic of SaaS?

a. Perpetual licensing

b. High maintenance costs

c. On-premise hosting

d. Automatic updates

Answer: d. Automatic updates.

5. Which of the following is a popular SaaS application used for email marketing?

a. Constant Contact

b. MailChimp

c. Aweber

d. Campaign Monitor

Answer: b. MailChimp.

6. Which of the following is a potential disadvantage of SaaS for businesses with limited internet connectivity?

a. Limited scalability

b. Higher upfront costs

c. Longer implementation time.

d. Limited accessibility

Answer: d. Limited accessibility.

17.   Which of the following is a characteristic of SaaS pricing?

   a. Upfront licensing fees

   b. Per-user pricing

   c. Perpetual licensing

   d. Local installation costs

Answer: b. Per-user pricing.

18.   Which of the following is a potential advantage of SaaS for businesses with multiple locations?

   a. Limited customization

   b. Higher upfront costs

   c. Longer implementation time

   d. Higher maintenance costs

Answer: a. Limited customization.

19.   Which of the following is a popular SaaS application used for customer support?

   a. Freshdesk

   b. Zendesk

c. Kayako

d. Help Scout

Answer: b. Zendesk.

0.   Which of the following is a potential disadvantage of SaaS for businesses with strict data privacy regulations?

a. Limited scalability.

b. Higher upfront costs

c. Compliance issues

d. Limited accessibility

Answer: c. Compliance issues.

21.   Which of the following is a characteristic of SaaS implementation?

a. Local installation

b. On-premise hosting

c. Cloud-based deployment

d. Perpetual licensing

Answer: c. Cloud-based deployment.

22.   Which of the following is a potential advantage of SaaS for businesses with limited IT resources?

a. Lower upfront costs

b. More customization options

c. Faster implementation time.

d. Greater control over the software

Answer: c. Faster implementation time.

23.   Which of the following is a popular SaaS application used for accounting?

a. QuickBooks Online

b. Xero

c. Wave

d. FreshBooks

Answer: a. QuickBooks Online.

24.   Which of the following is a potential disadvantage of SaaS for businesses with high customization requirements?

a. Limited scalability

b. Higher upfront costs.

c. Longer implementation time

d. Limited customization options

Answer: d. Limited customization options.

25.   Which of the following is a characteristic of SaaS support?

a. On-site technical support

b. Phone-based support

c. Email-based support.

d. Self-service support

Answer: d. Self-service support.

26.   Which of the following is a popular SaaS application used for team communication?

   a. Microsoft Teams.

   b. Slack

   c. Zoom

   d. Google Meet

Answer: b. Slack.

27.   Which of the following is a potential advantage of SaaS for businesses with limited storage space?

   a. Lower upfront costs

   b. More customization options

   c. Faster implementation time

   d. No local installation required

Answer: d. No local installation required.

28.   Which of the following is a potential disadvantage of SaaS for businesses with limited internet bandwidth?

   a. Limited scalability

   b. Higher upfront costs

c. Longer implementation time

d. Slow software performance

Answer: d. Slow software performance.

29.   Which of the following is a characteristic of SaaS updates?

a. User-initiated updates

b. On-premise updates

c. Automatic updates

d. Manual updates

Answer: c. Automatic updates.

30.   Which of the following is a popular SaaS application used for social media management?

a. Hootsuite

b. Sprout Social

c. Buffer.

d. Later

Answer: a. Hootsuite.

31.   Which of the following is a potential advantage of SaaS for businesses with international teams?

a. Lower upfront costs

b. More customization options

c. Faster implementation time

d. Easy collaboration across time zones

Answer: d. Easy collaboration across time zones.

32.   Which of the following is a potential disadvantage of SaaS for businesses with complex IT infrastructures?

a. Limited scalability.

b. Higher upfront costs.

c. Longer implementation time

d. Limited integration options

Answer: d. Limited integration options.

33.   Which of the following is a characteristic of SaaS availability?

a. Limited availability

b. On-premise hosting

c. 24/7 availability

d. User-initiated availability

Answer: c. 24/7 availability.

34.   Which of the following is a popular SaaS application used for project accounting?

a. Harvest

b. Mavenlink

c. BigTime

d. Accelo.

Answer: a. Harvest.

35.   Which of the following is a potential advantage of SaaS for businesses with remote workers?

   a. Lower upfront costs

   b. More customization options

   c. Faster implementation time

   d. Easy access to software from anywhere with an internet connection

Answer: d. Easy access to software from anywhere with an internet connection.

36.   Which of the following is a potential disadvantage of SaaS for businesses with high data storage needs?

   a. Limited scalability

   b. Higher upfront costs

   c. Longer implementation time d. Limited storage options Answer: d. Limited storage options.

37.   Which of the following is a characteristic of SaaS security?

   a. On-premise security

   b. User-initiated security

   c. Cloud-based security

d. Perpetual security

Answer: c. Cloud-based security.

8.   Which of the following is a popular SaaS application used for customer feedback management?

a. SurveyMonkey

b. Qualtrics

c. Typeform

d. SurveyGizmo

Answer: b. Qualtrics.

39.   Which of the following is a potential advantage of SaaS for businesses with limited hardware resources?

a. Lower upfront costs

b. More customization options

c. Faster implementation time.

d. Reduced hardware requirements

Answer: d. Reduced hardware requirements.

40.   Which of the following is a potential disadvantage of SaaS for businesses with strict service level agreements?

a. Limited scalability.

b. Higher upfront costs

c. Longer implementation time

d. Limited-service level agreement options.

Answer: d. Limited-service level agreement options.

41.	Which of the following is a characteristic of SaaS data management?

a. On-premise data management

b. User-initiated data management

c. Cloud-based data management

d. Perpetual data management

Answer: c. Cloud-based data management.

42.	Which of the following is a popular SaaS application used for applicant tracking?

a. Lever.

b. Greenhouse.

c. Workable.

d. JazzHR

Answer: b. Greenhouse.

43.	Which of the following is a potential advantage of SaaS for businesses with limited software expertise?

a. Lower upfront costs

b. More customization options

c. Faster implementation time

d. Reduced software expertise requirements

Answer: d. Reduced software expertise requirements.

44.   Which of the following is a potential disadvantage of SaaS for businesses with strict data retention policies?

a. Limited scalability.

b. Higher upfront costs

c. Longer implementation time

d. Limited data retention options

Answer: d. Limited data retention options.

45.   Which of the following is a characteristic of SaaS uptime?

a. Limited uptime

b. On-premise hosting.

c. High uptime.

d. User-initiated uptime

Answer: c. High uptime.

46.   Which of the following is a popular SaaS application used for web analytics?

a. Google Analytics

b. Adobe Analytics

c. Mixpanel

d. Piwik PRO

Answer: a. Google Analytics.

47.   Which of the following is a potential advantage of SaaS for businesses with limited physical office space?

a. Lower upfront costs

b. More customization options

c. Faster implementation time

d. Reduced physical office space requirements

Answer: d. Reduced physical office space requirements.

48.   Which of the following is a potential disadvantage of SaaS for businesses with high user volume?

a. Limited scalability

b. Higher upfront costs

c. Longer implementation time

d. Limited user volume options

Answer: a. Limited scalability.

49.   Which of the following is a characteristic of SaaS compliance?

a. On-premise compliance

b. User-initiated compliance

c. Cloud-based compliance.

d. None of the above.

Answer: c. Cloud-based compliance.

50.   Which of the following is a popular SaaS application used for video conferencing?

a. Skype.

b. GoToMeeting

c. Cisco Webex.

d. Blue Jeans

Answer: c. Cisco Webex.

Printed in Great Britain
by Amazon

27295536R00030